⭐ Amazing
WildLife
Adult Coloring Book

Copyright 2020 by Arthur Little

All rights reserved. This book or any portion thereof may not be reproduced or used in any manner whatsoever without express written permission of the publisher excepts for the use of brief quotations in a book review.

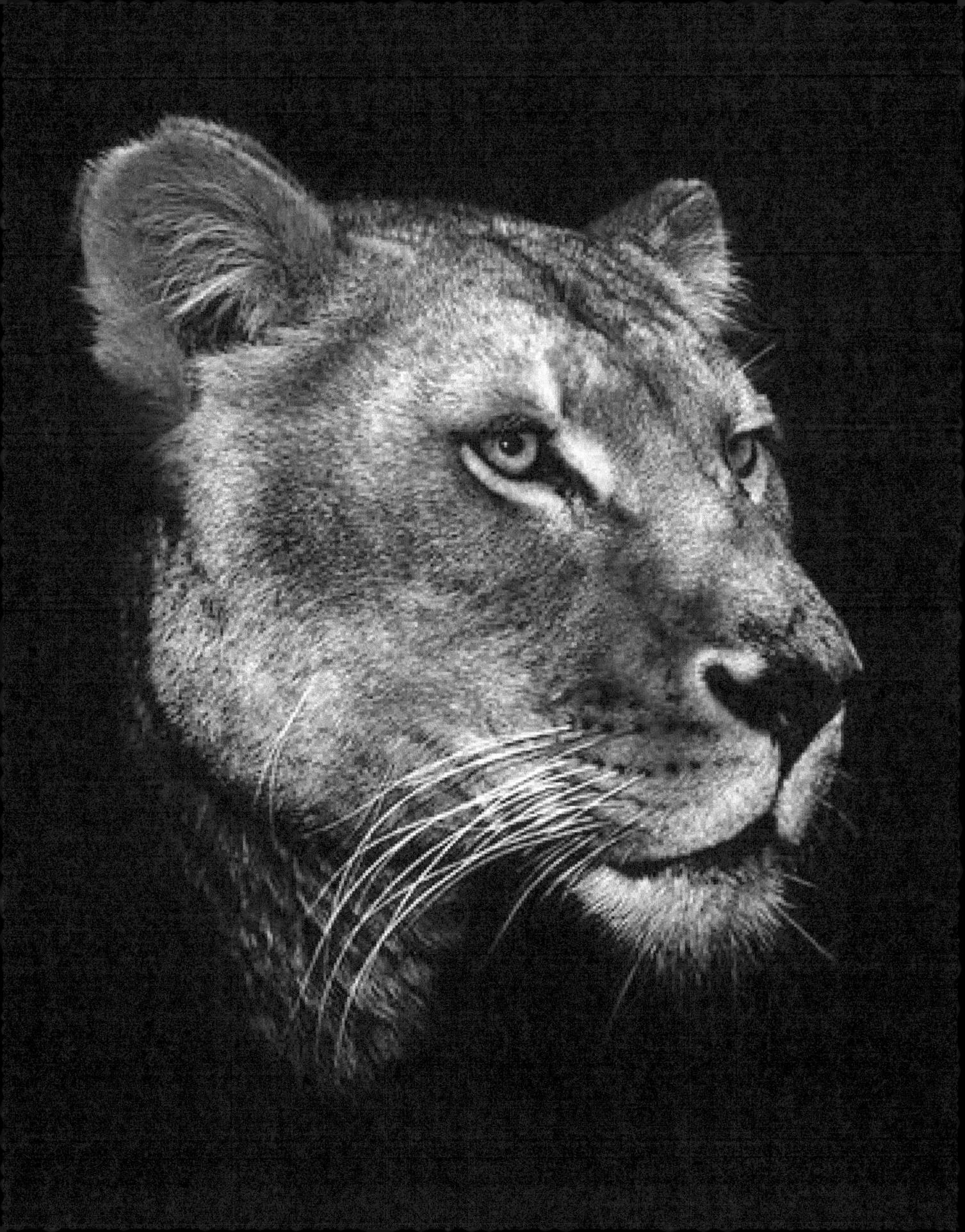

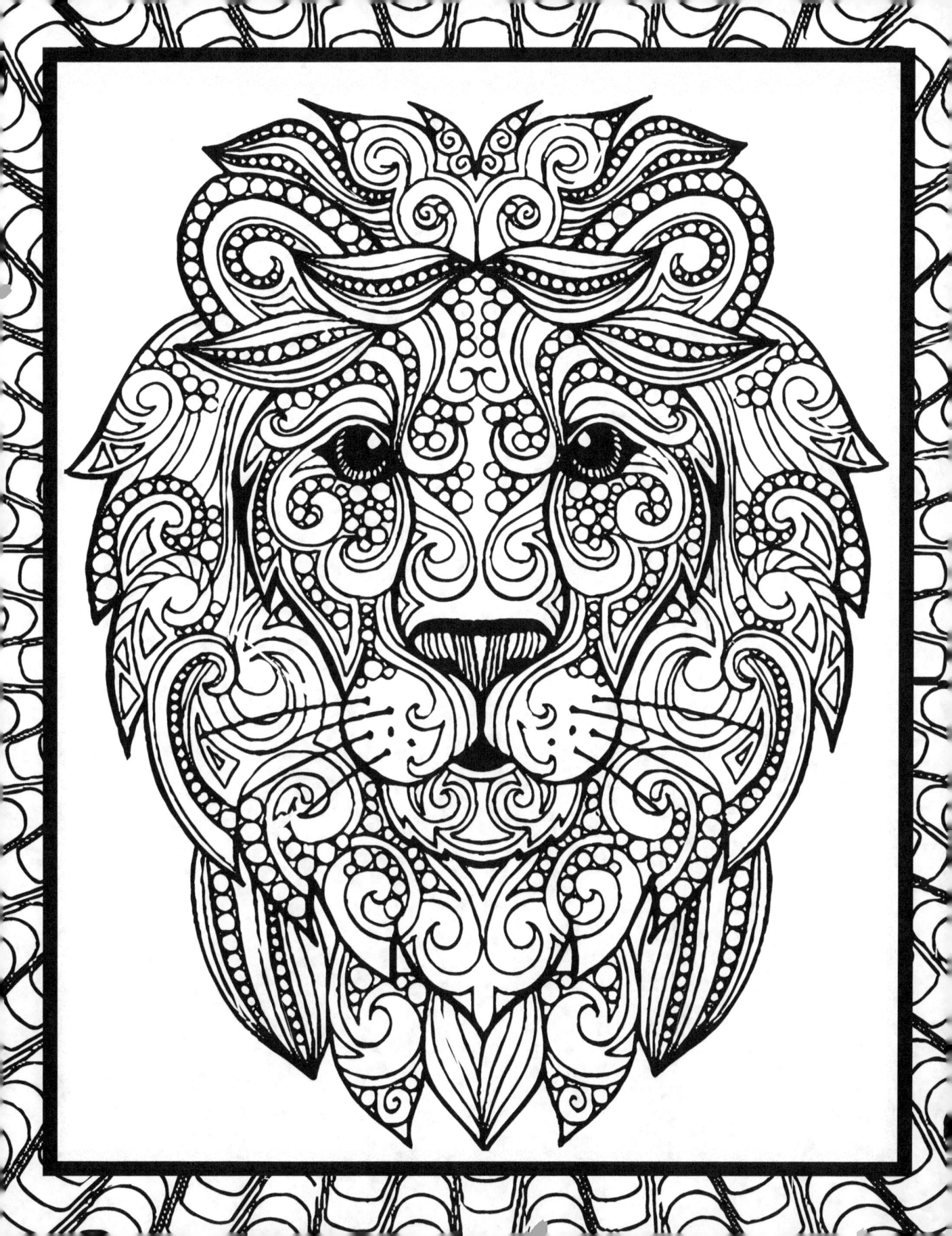

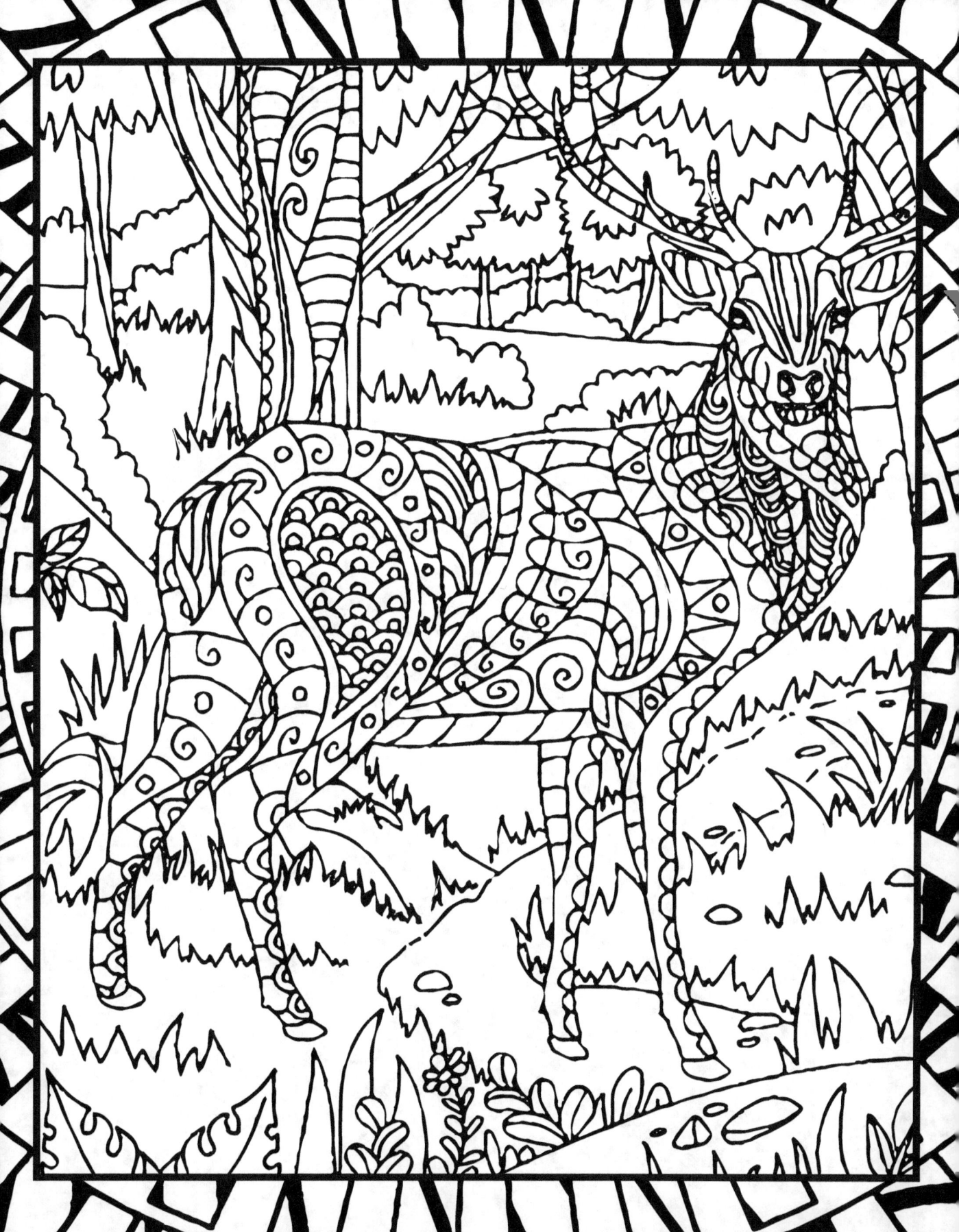

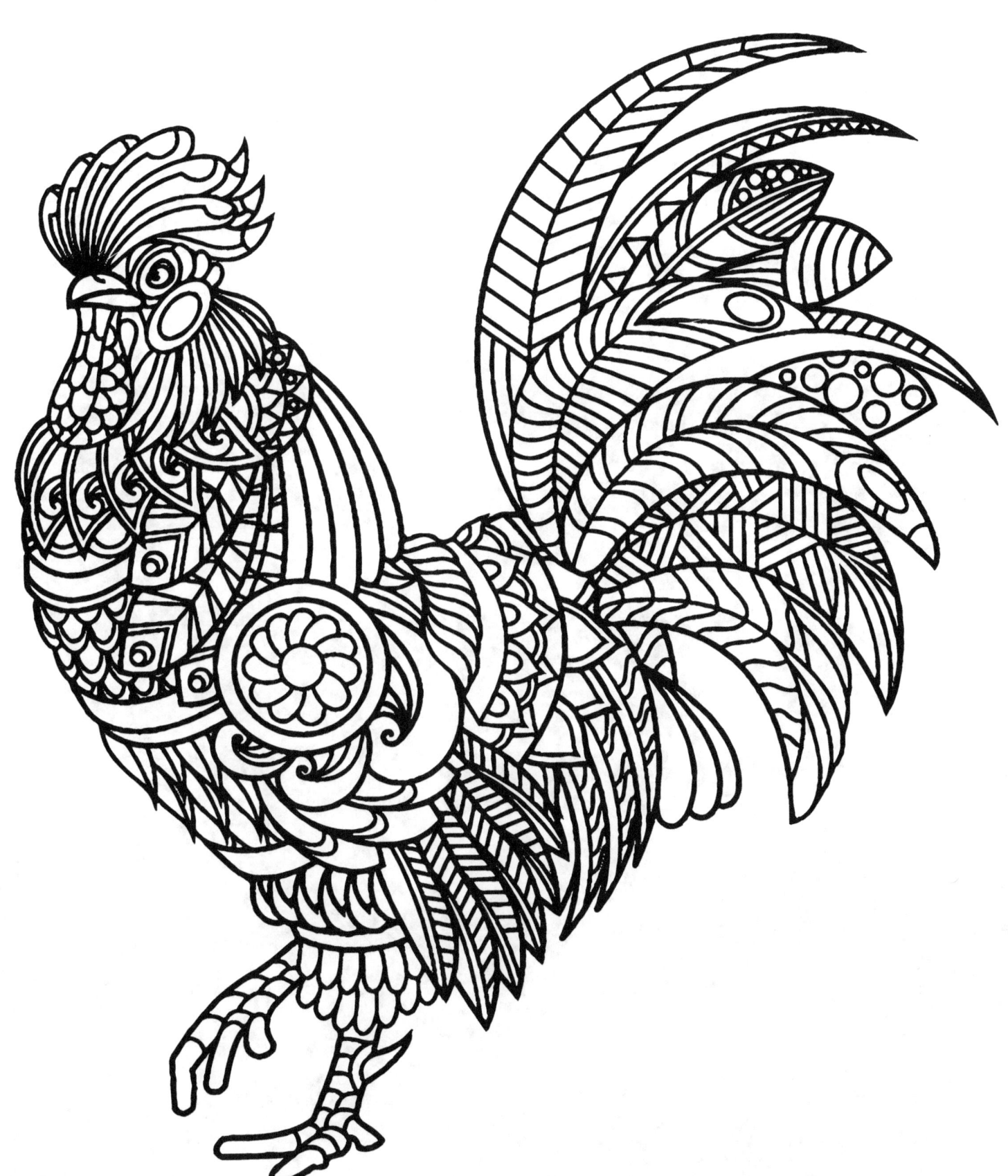

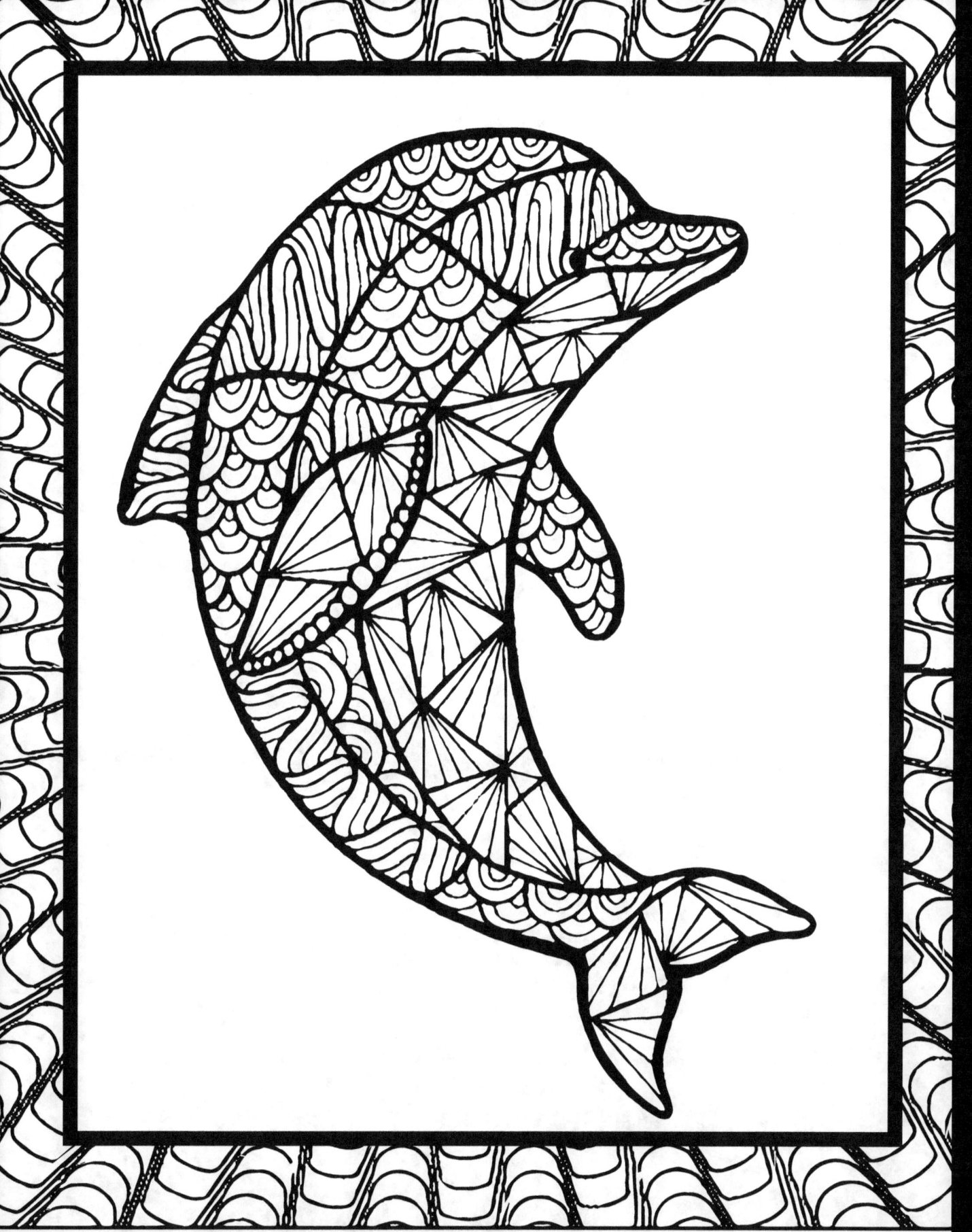

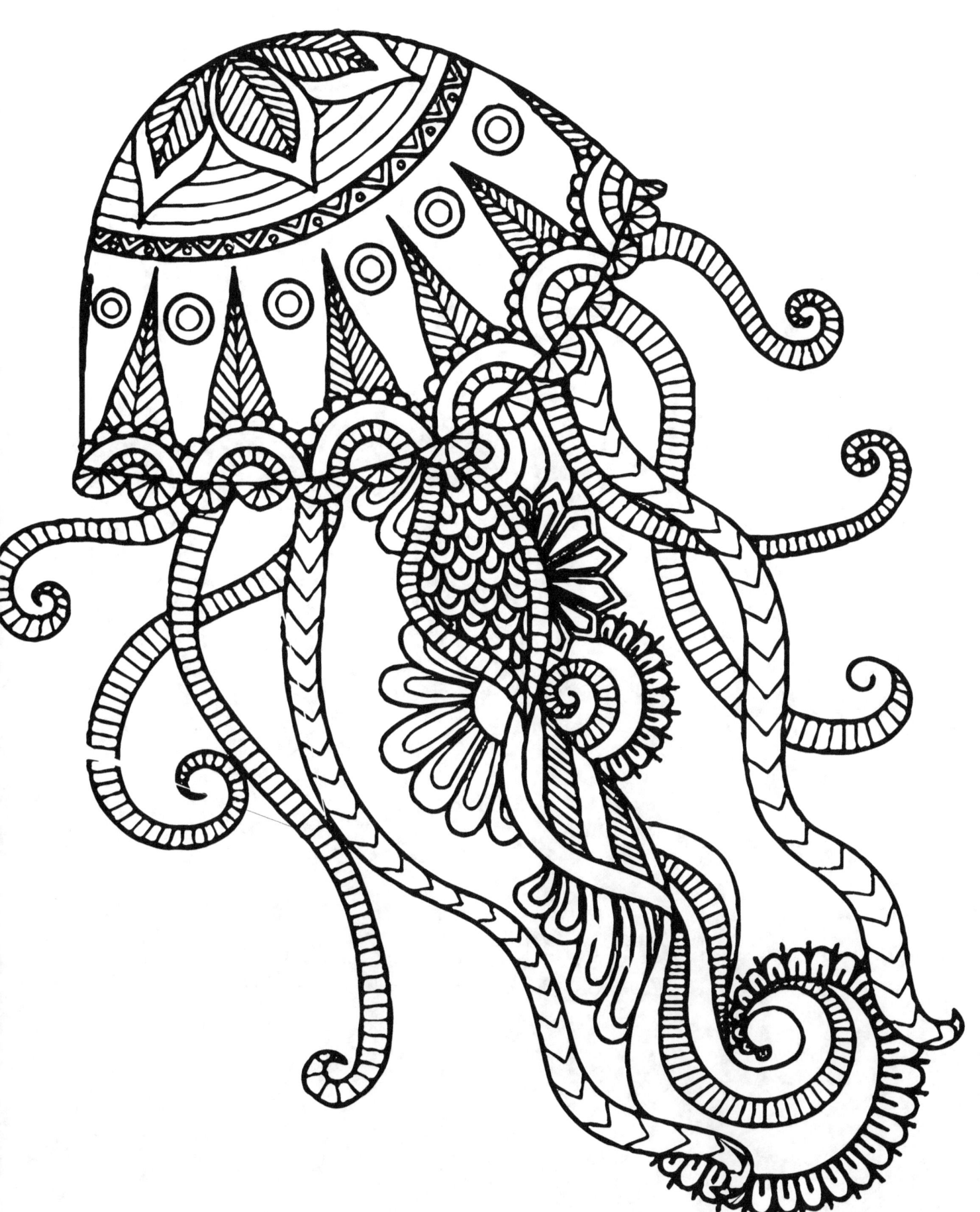

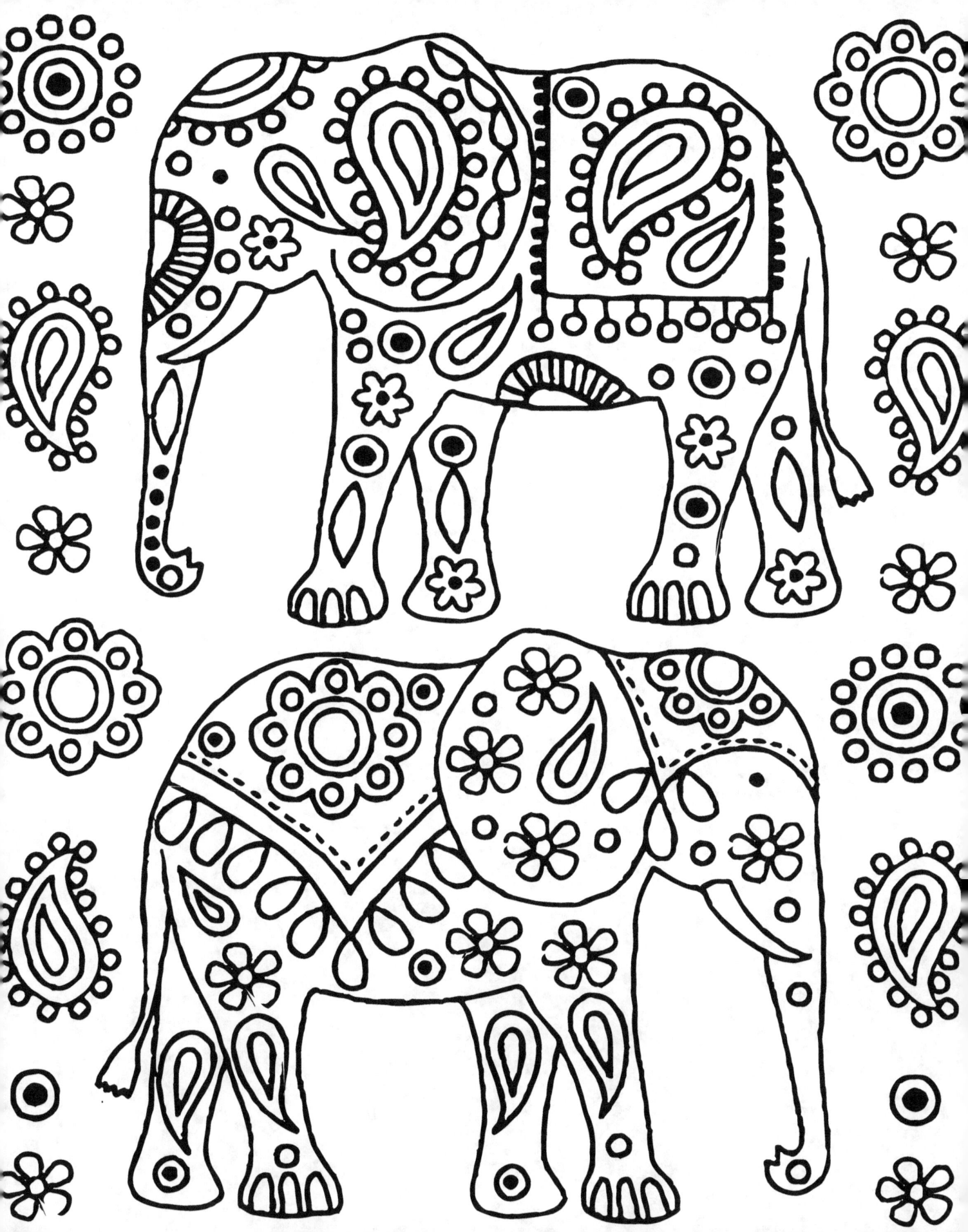

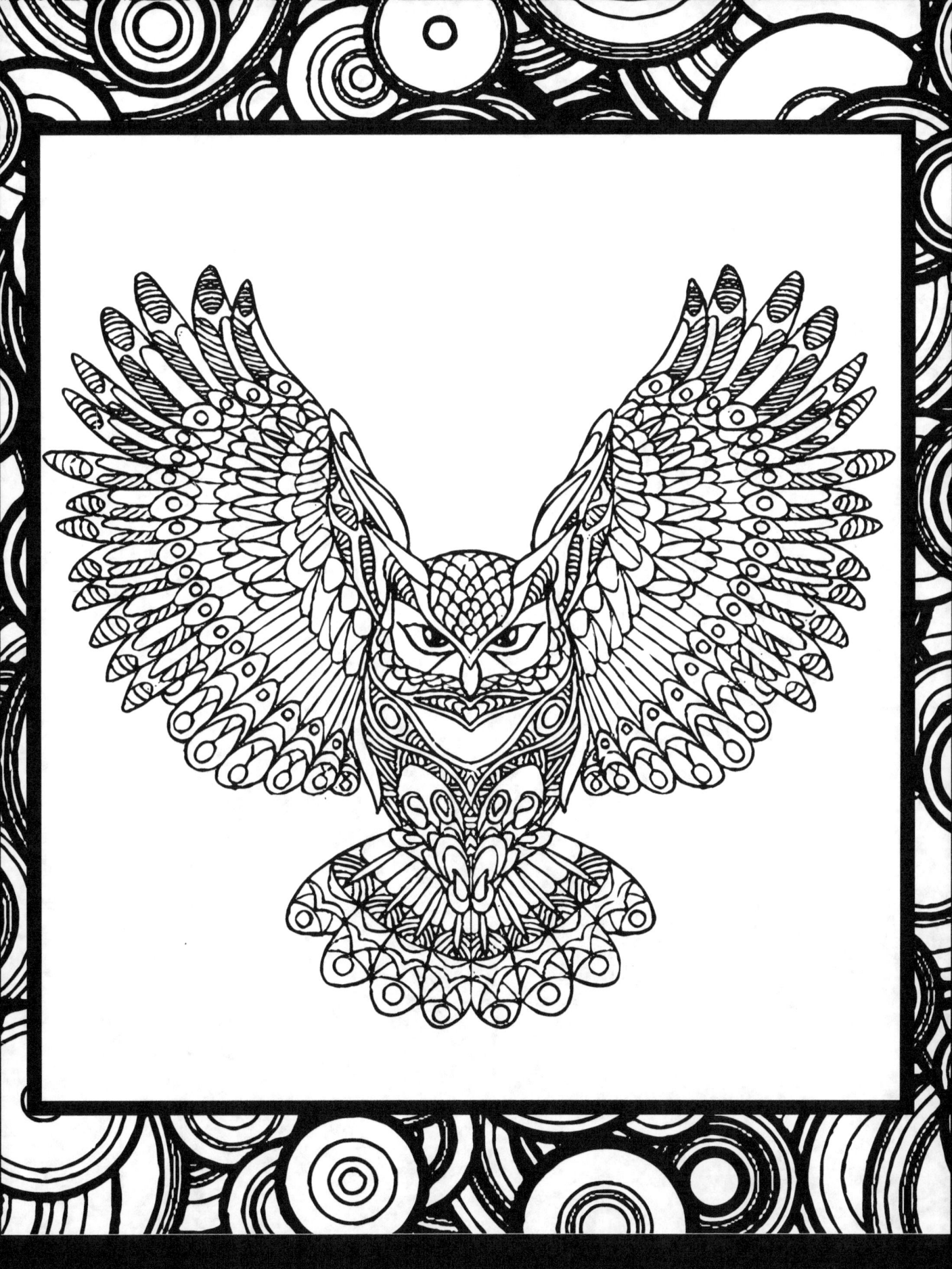

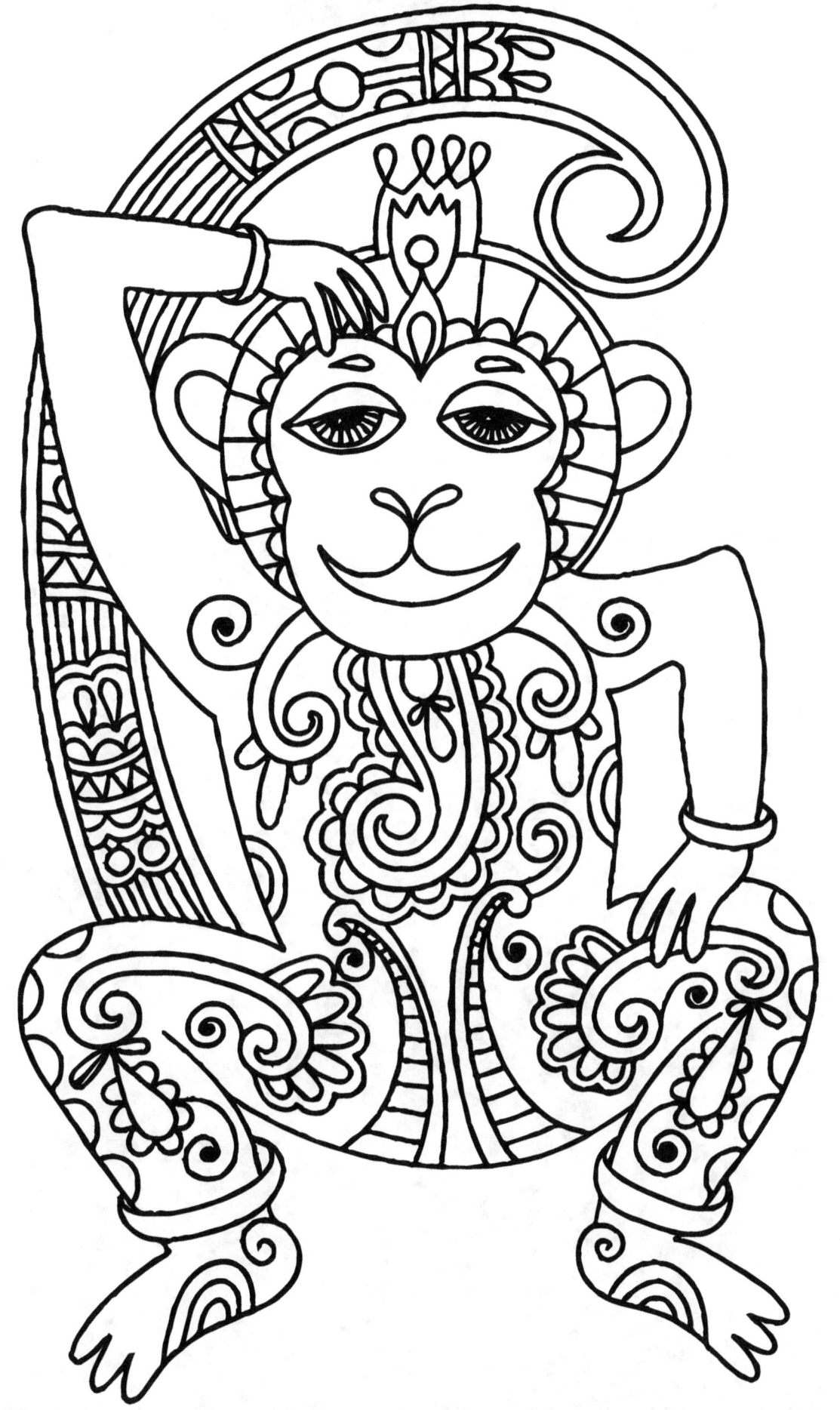

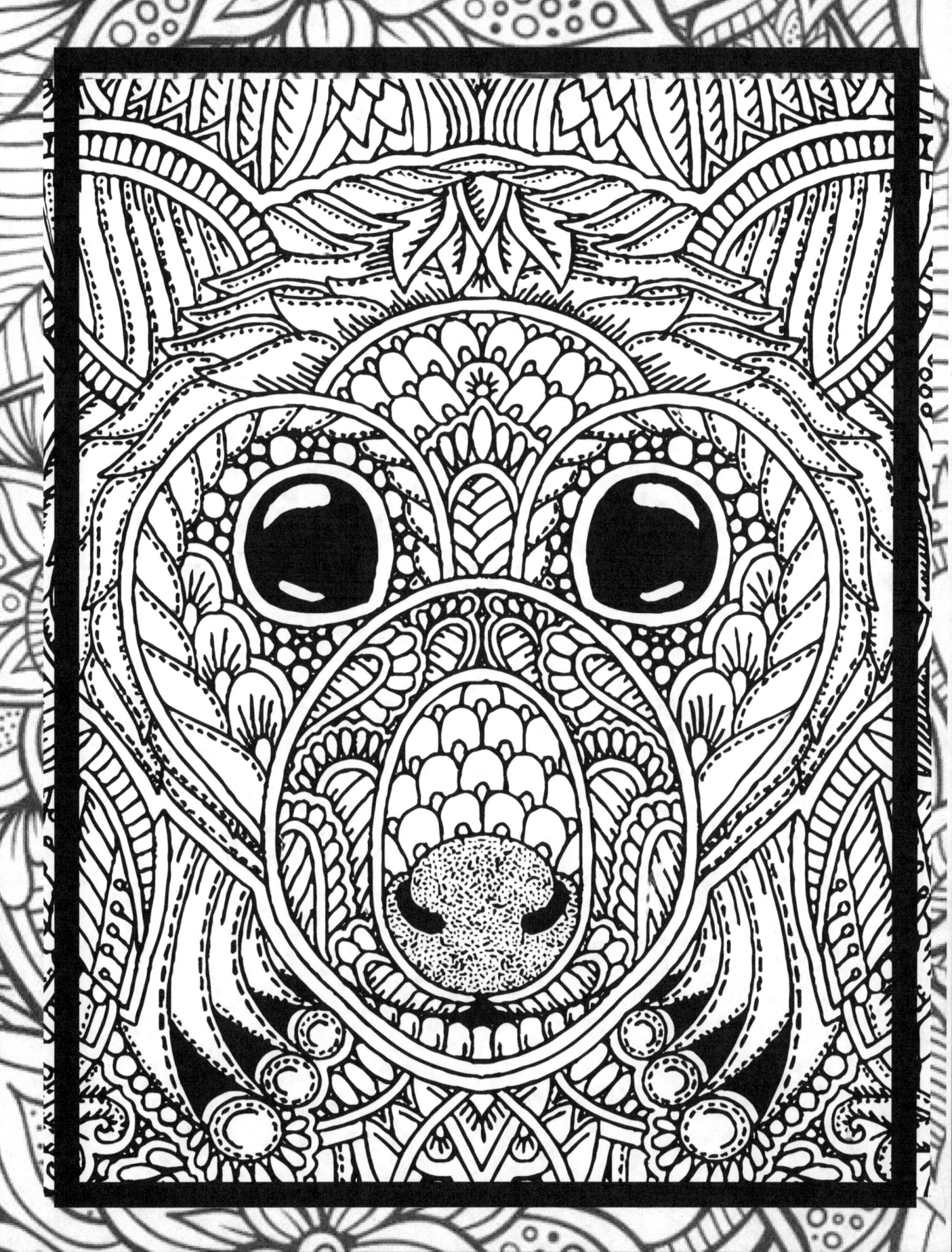

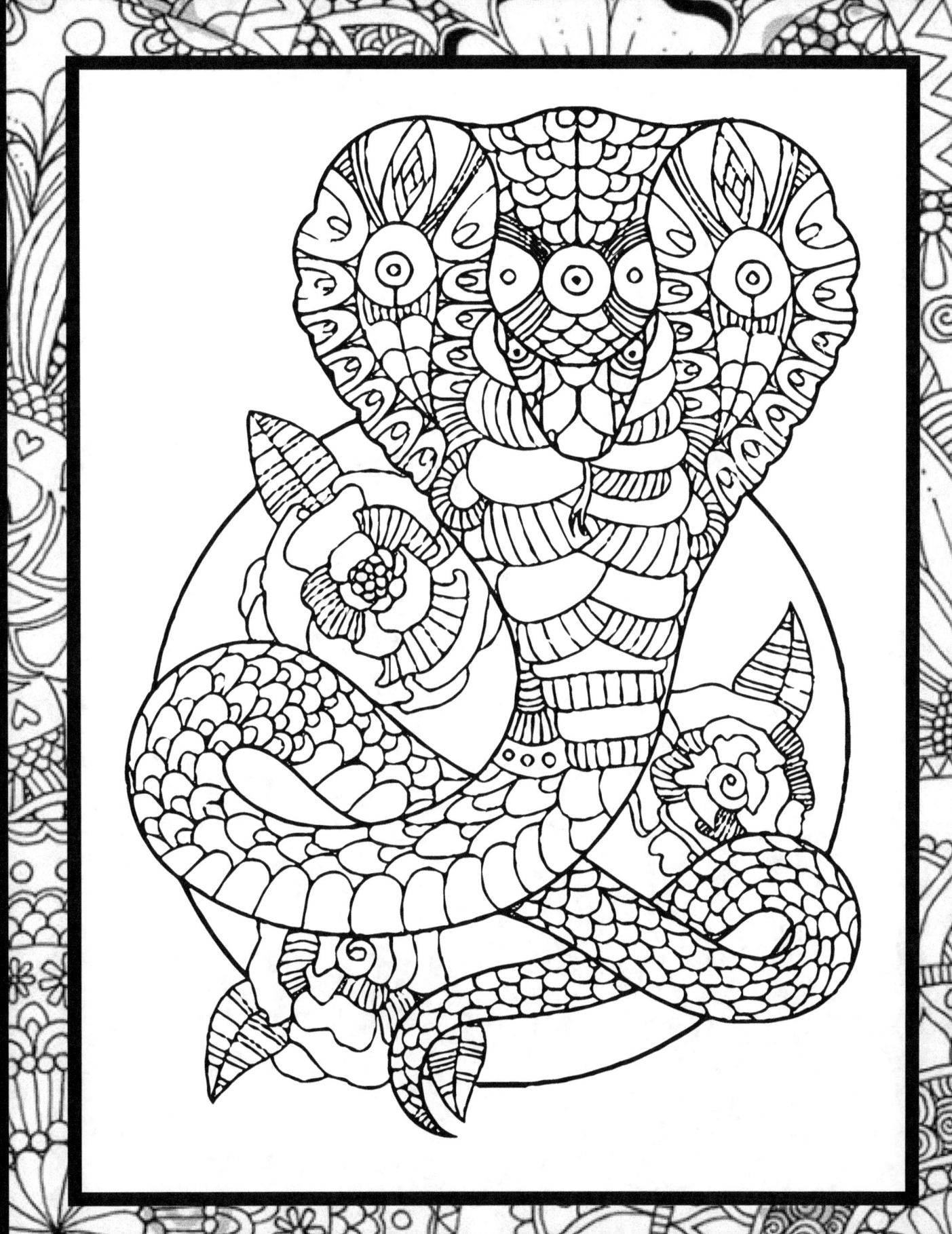

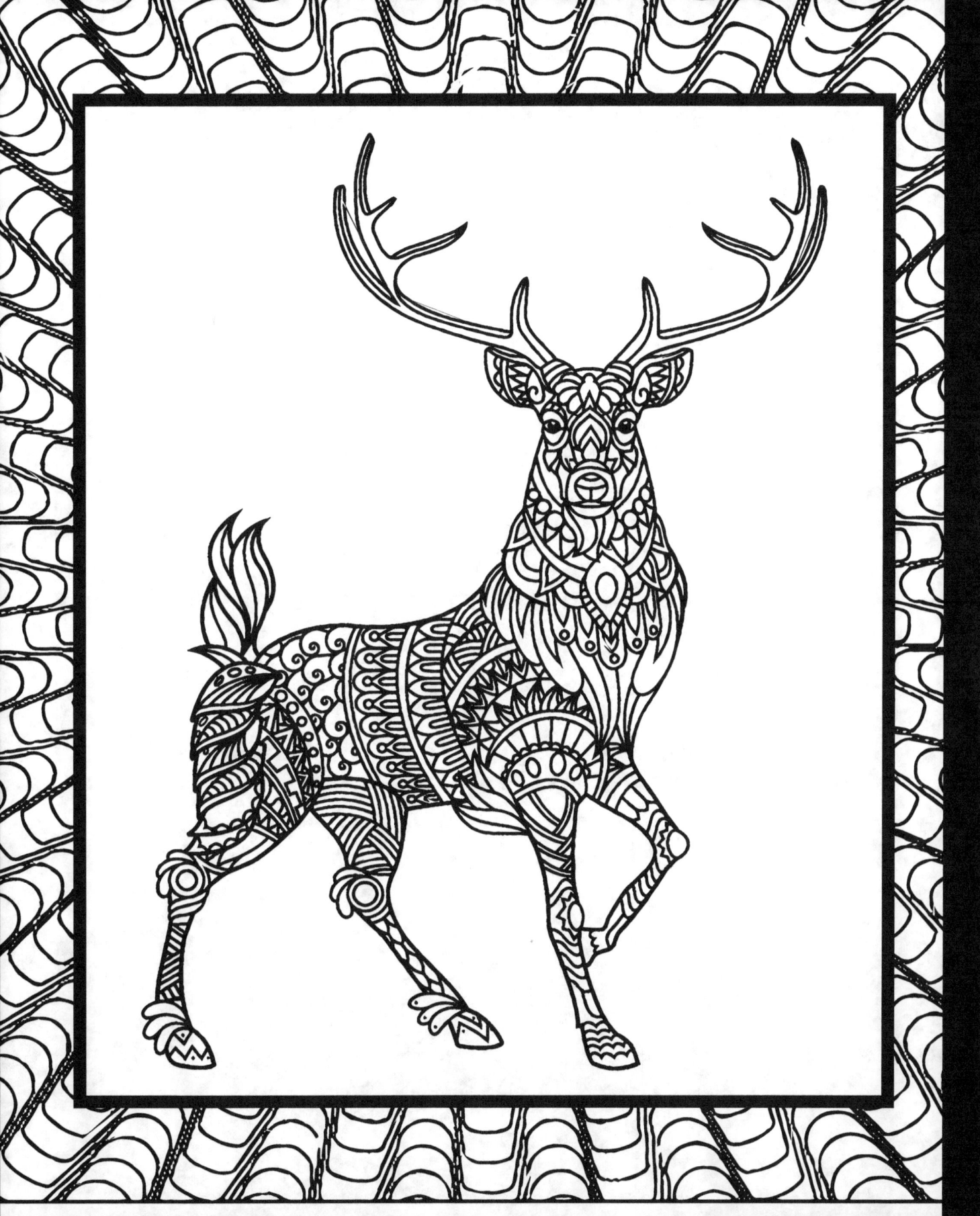

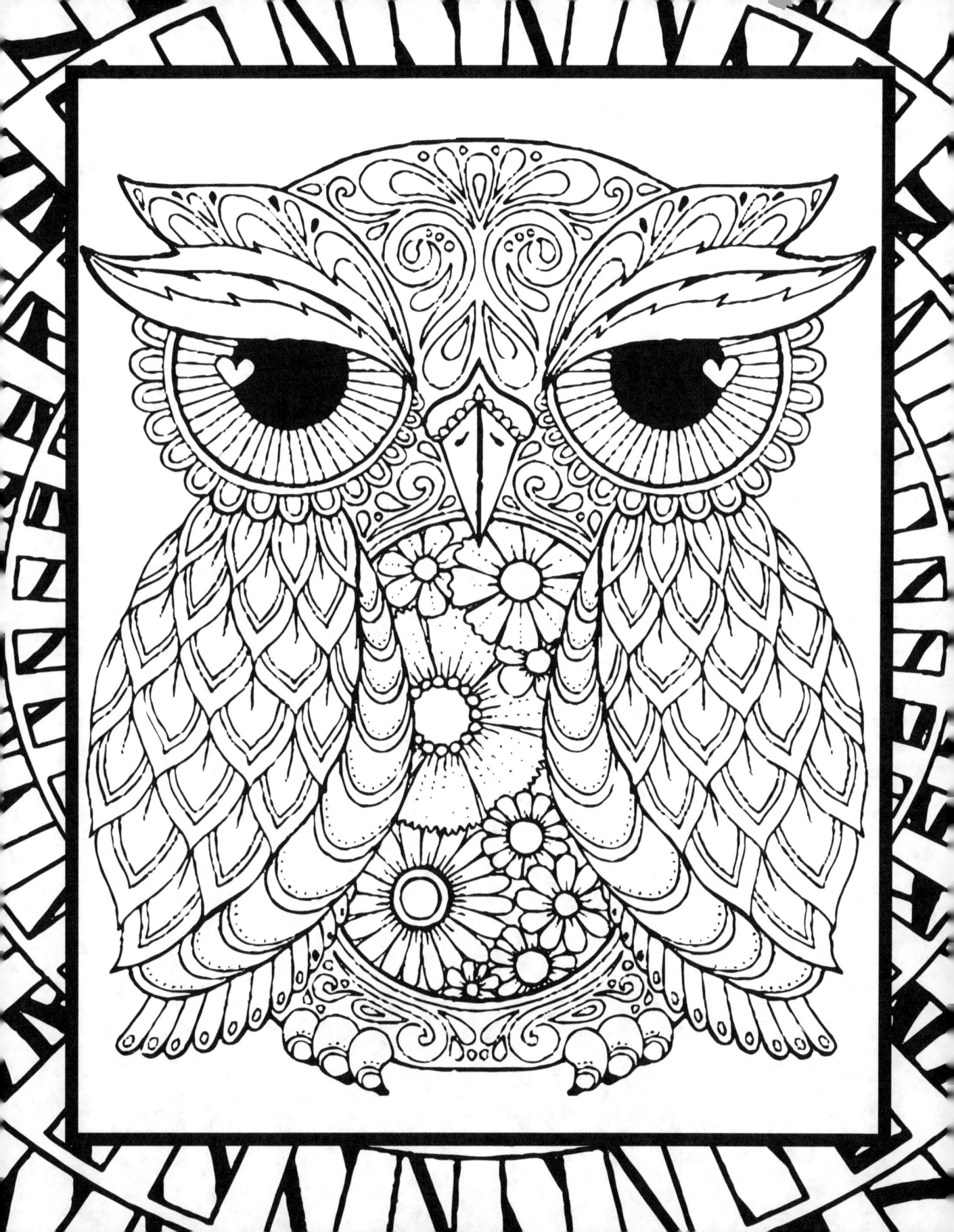

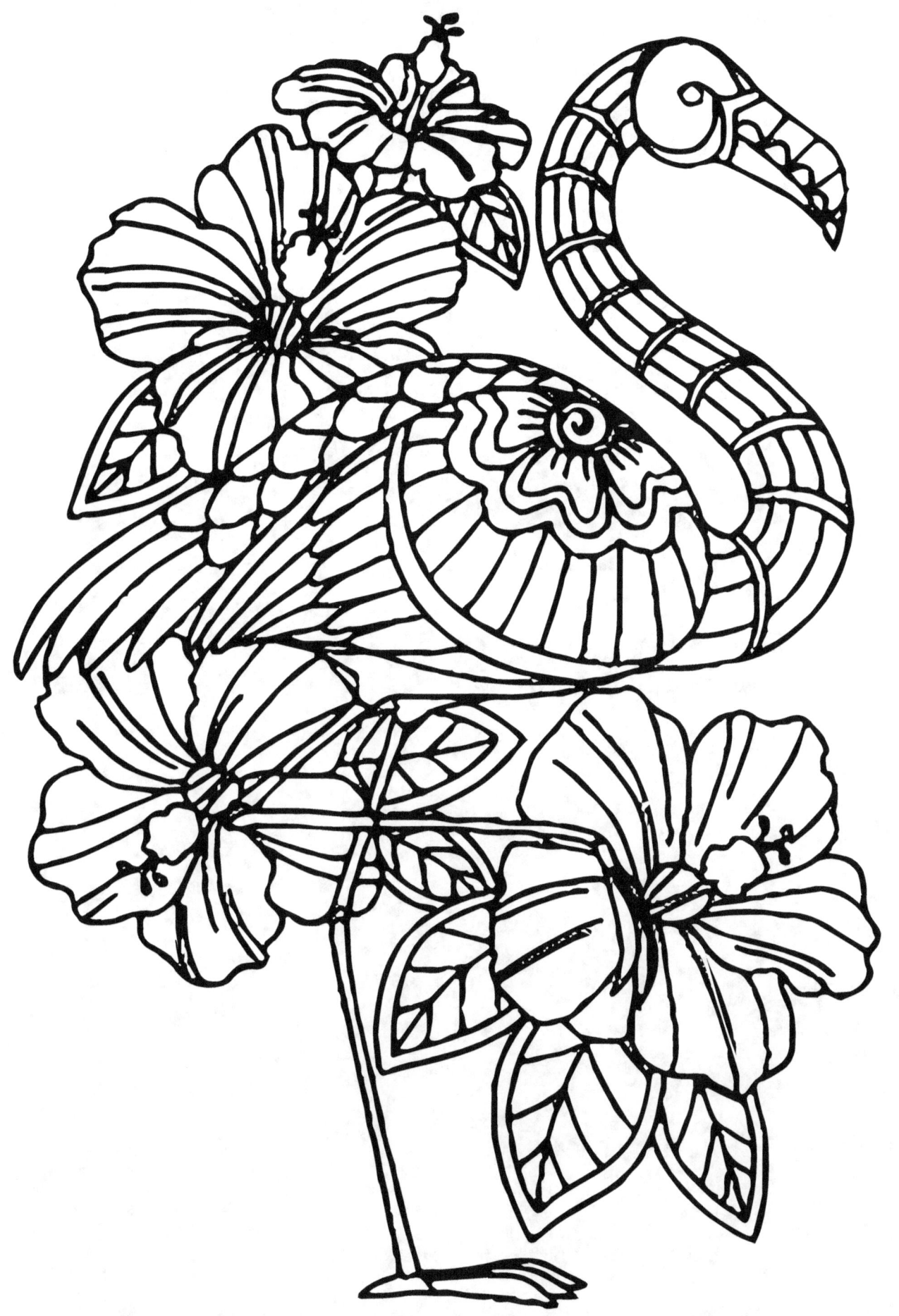

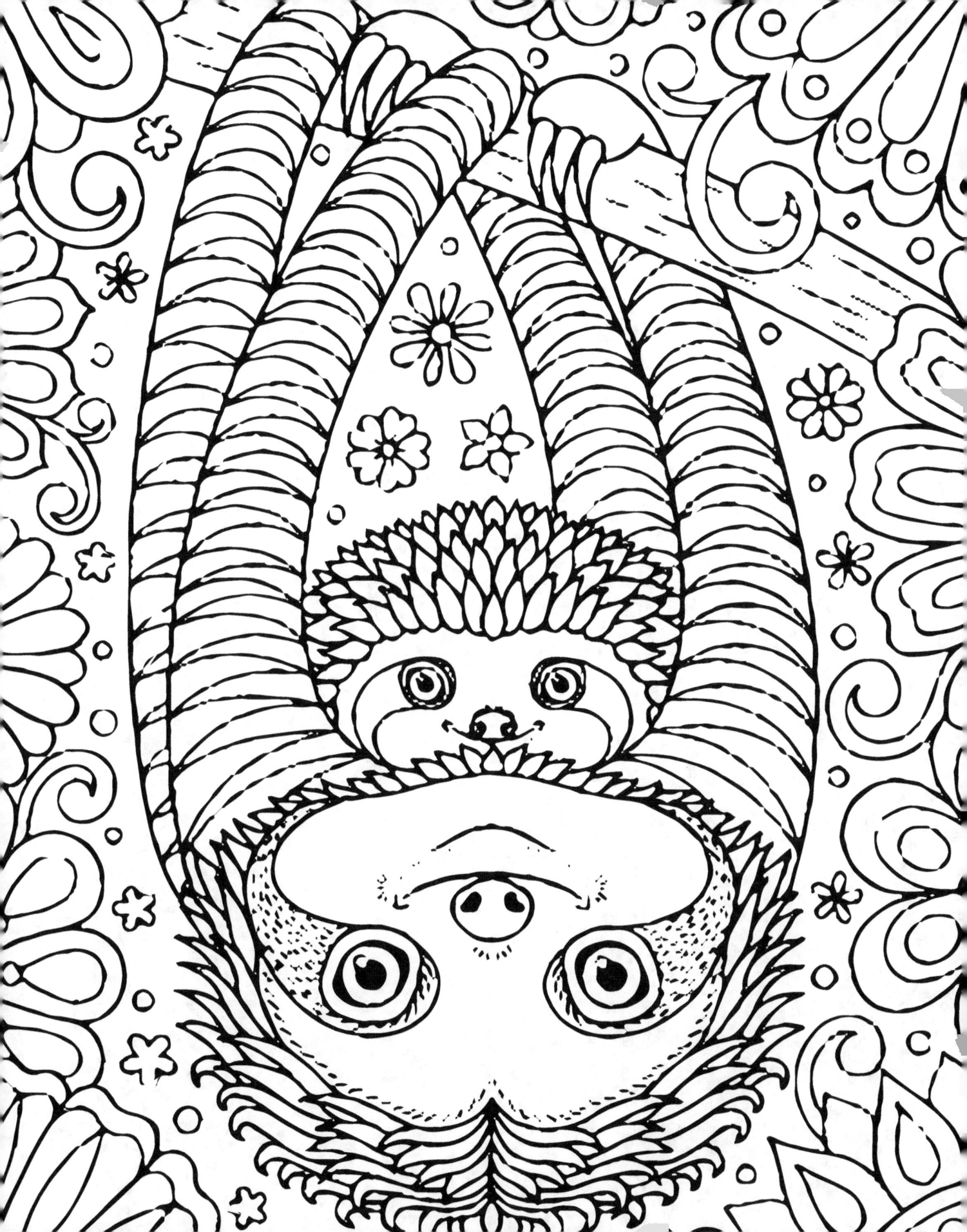

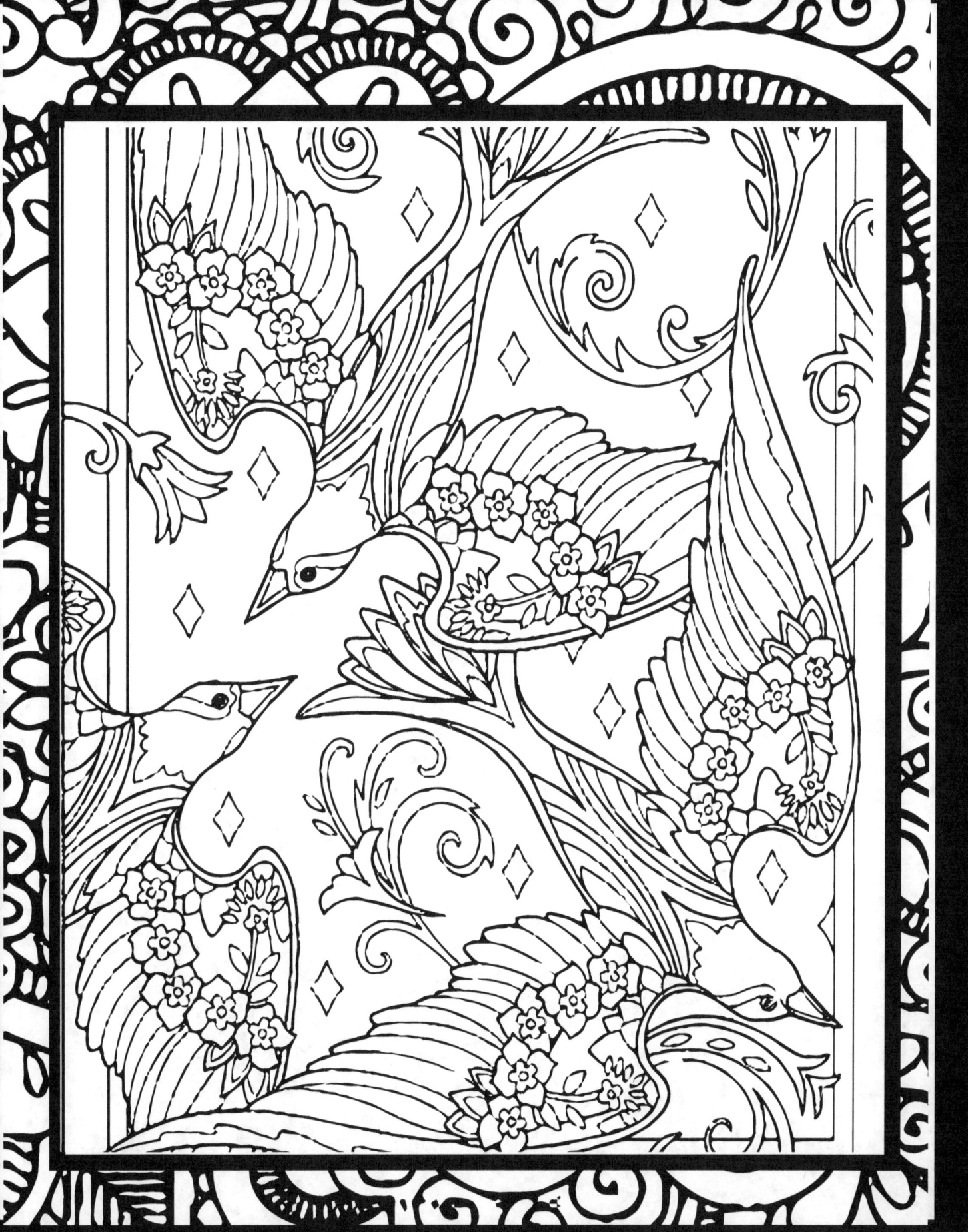

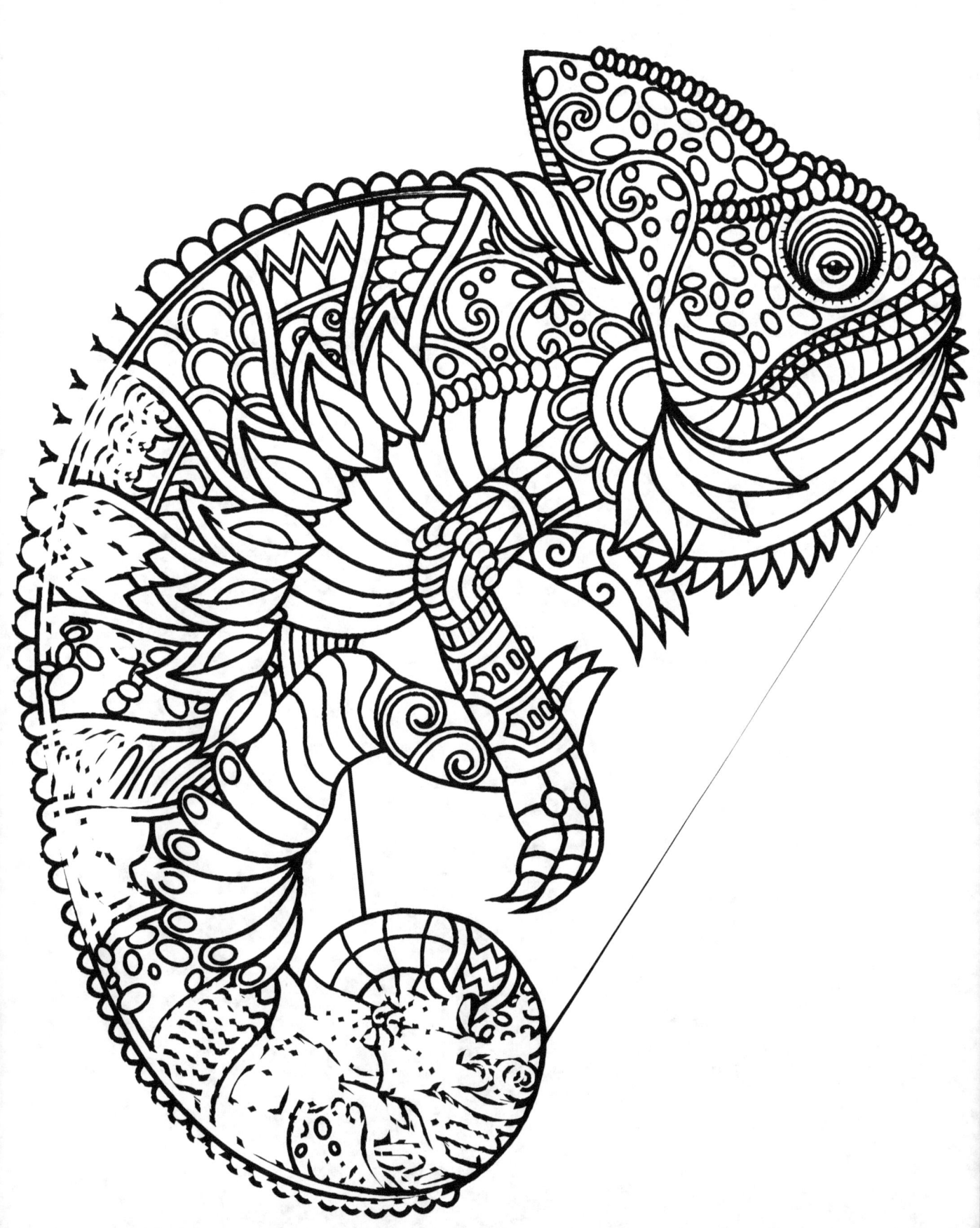

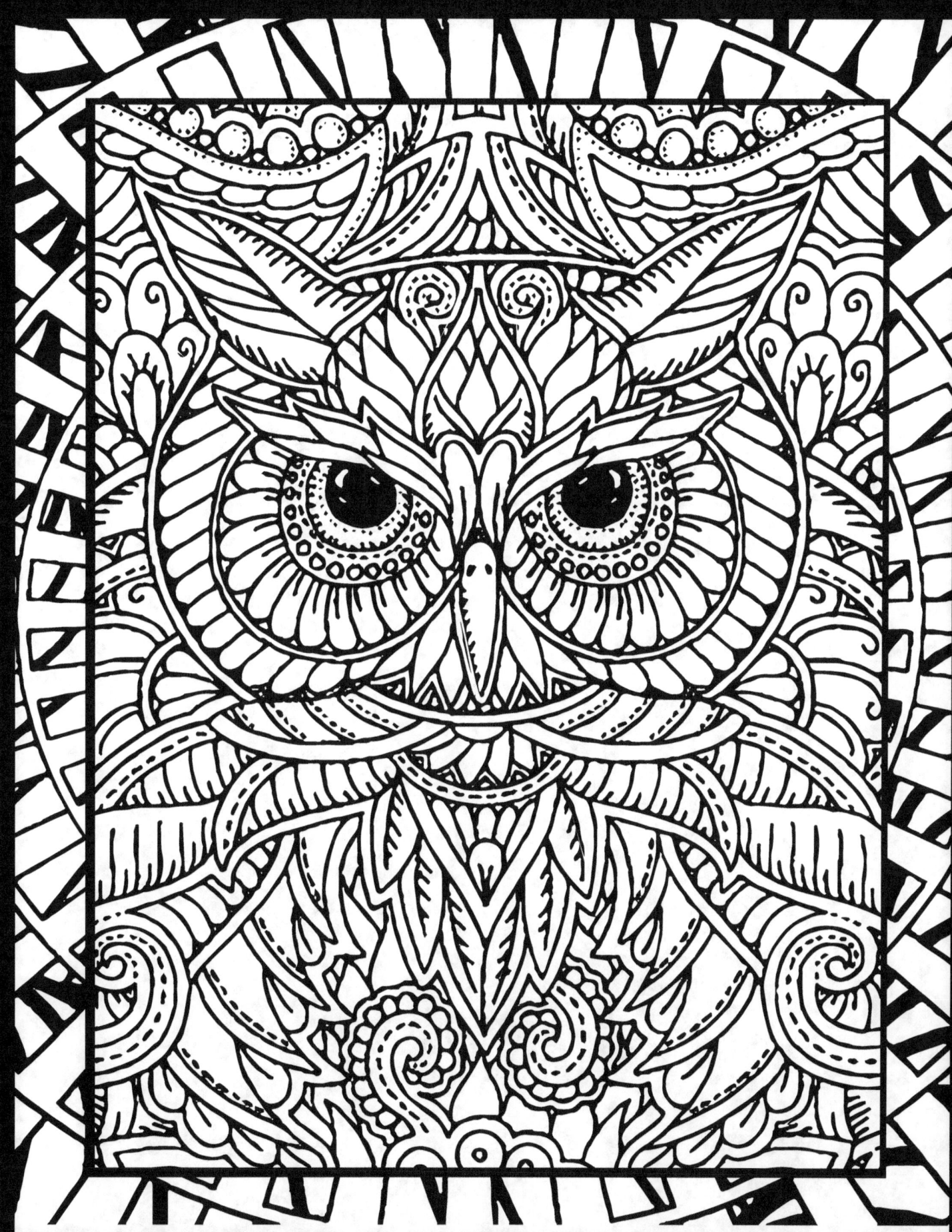

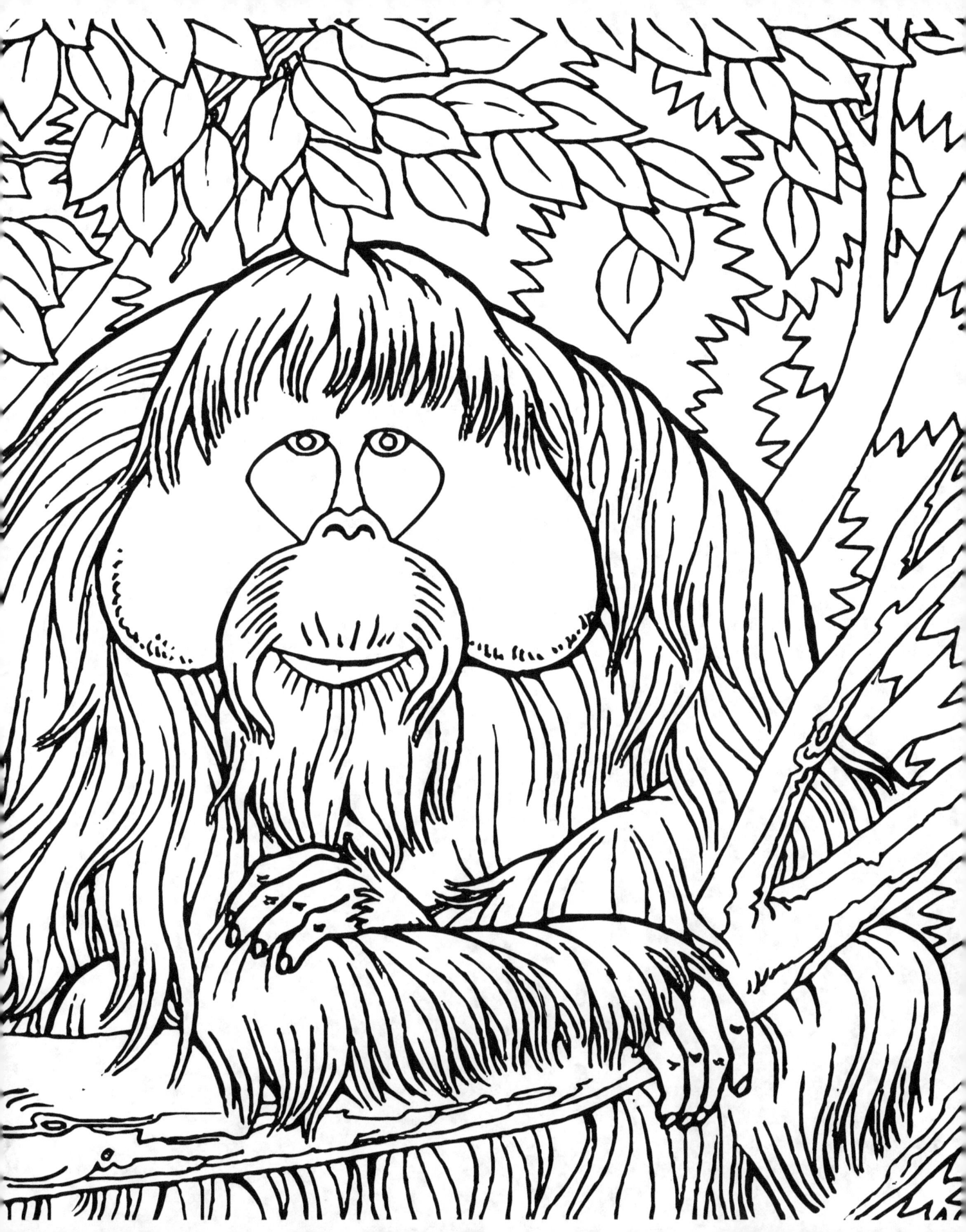

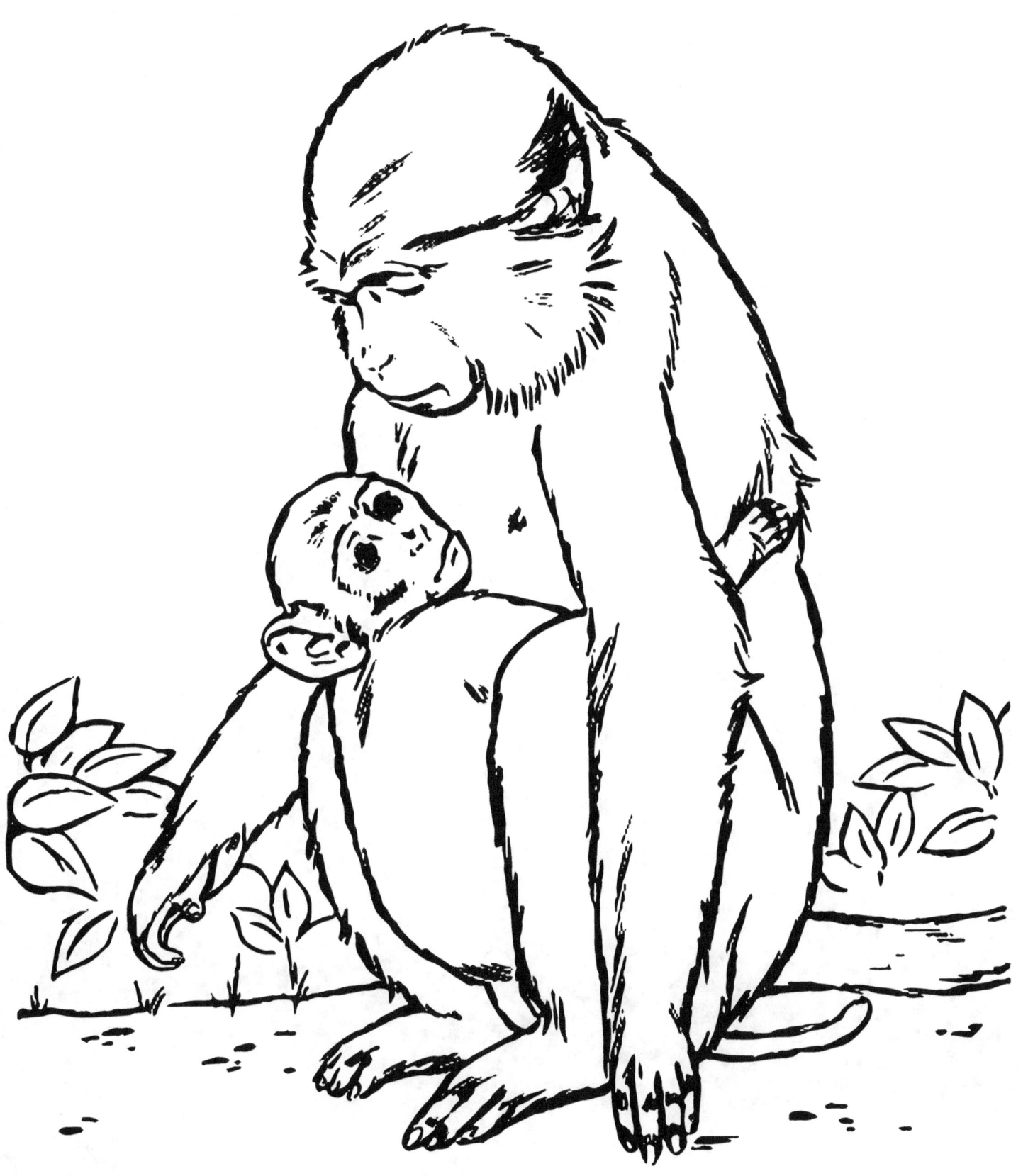

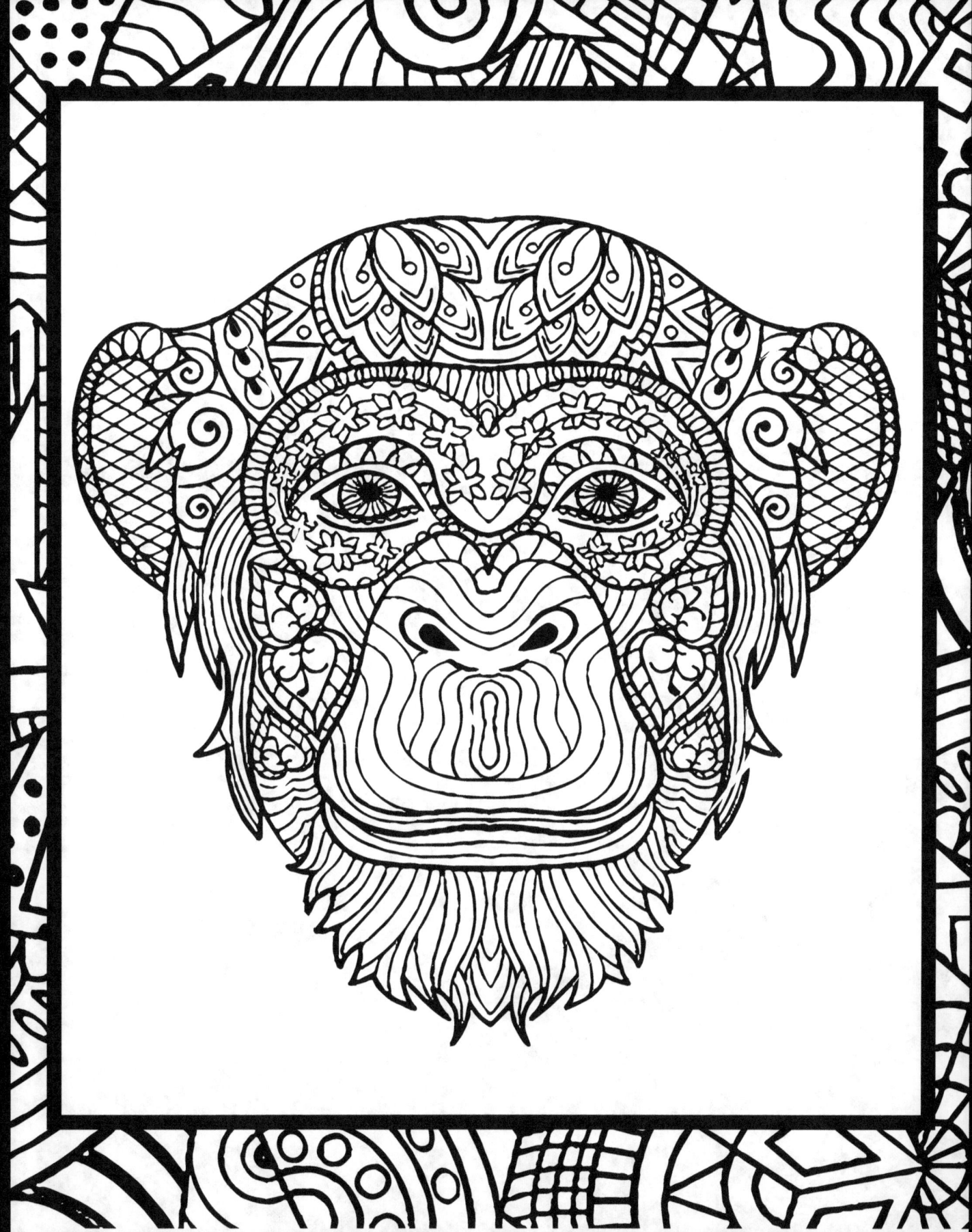

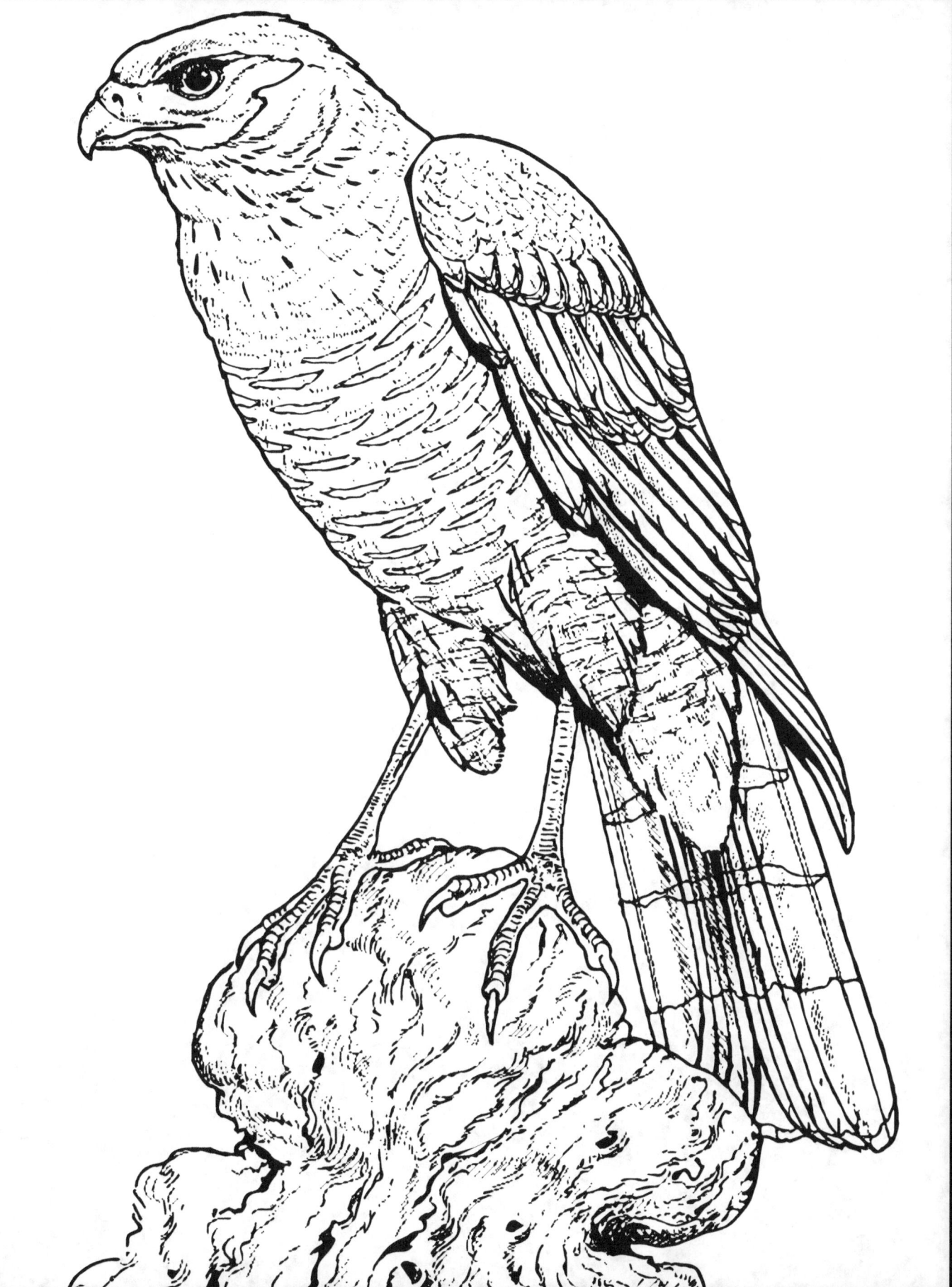

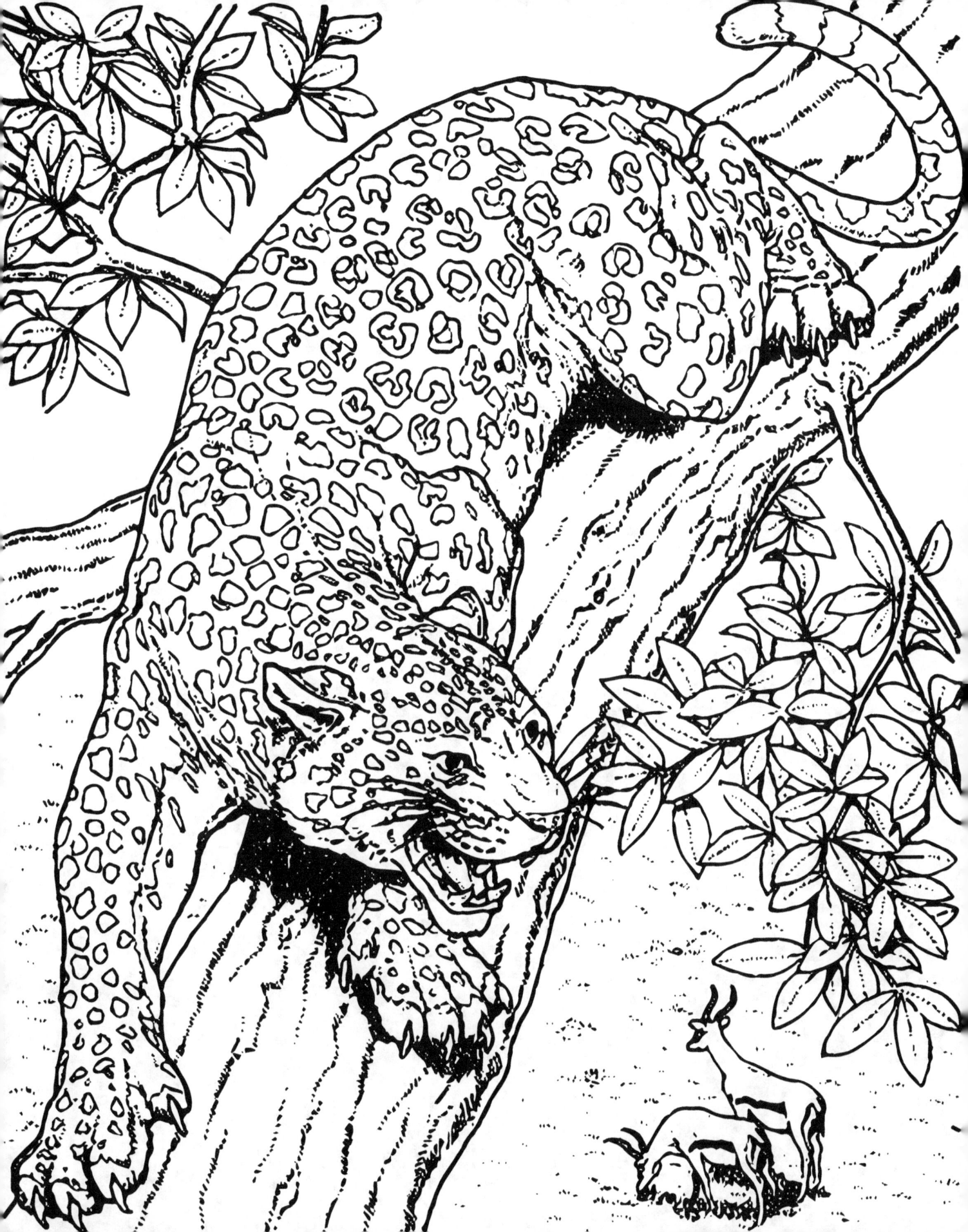

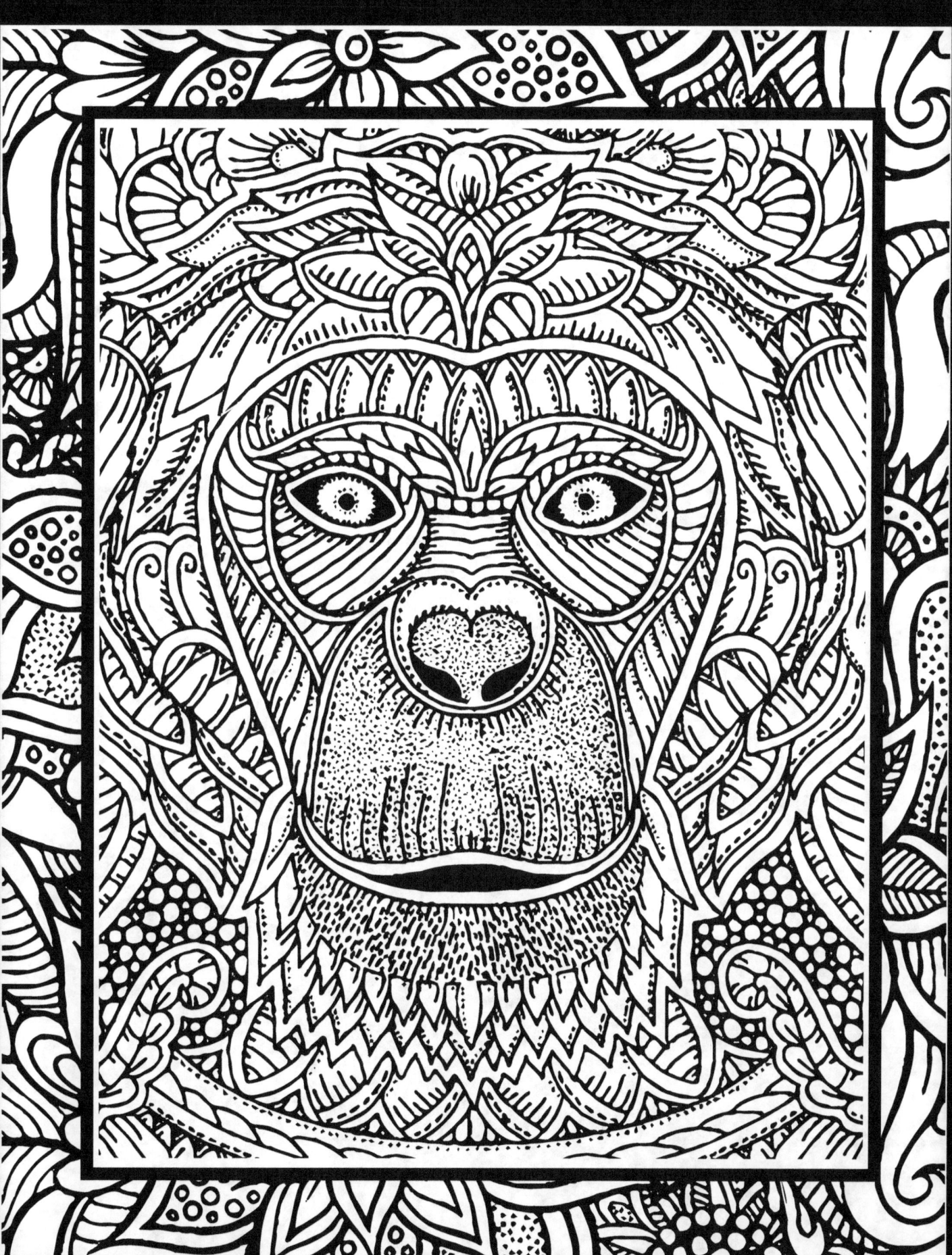

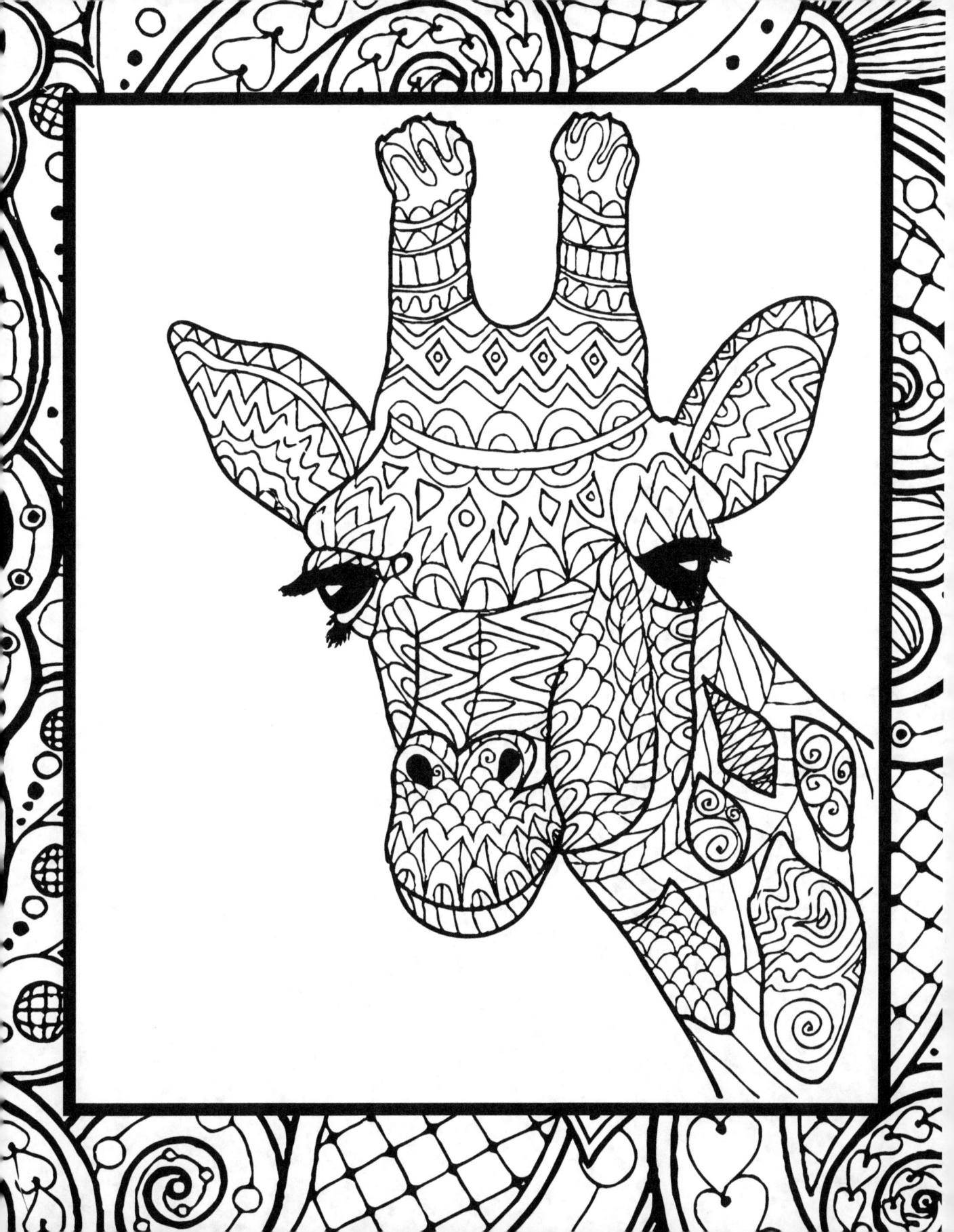

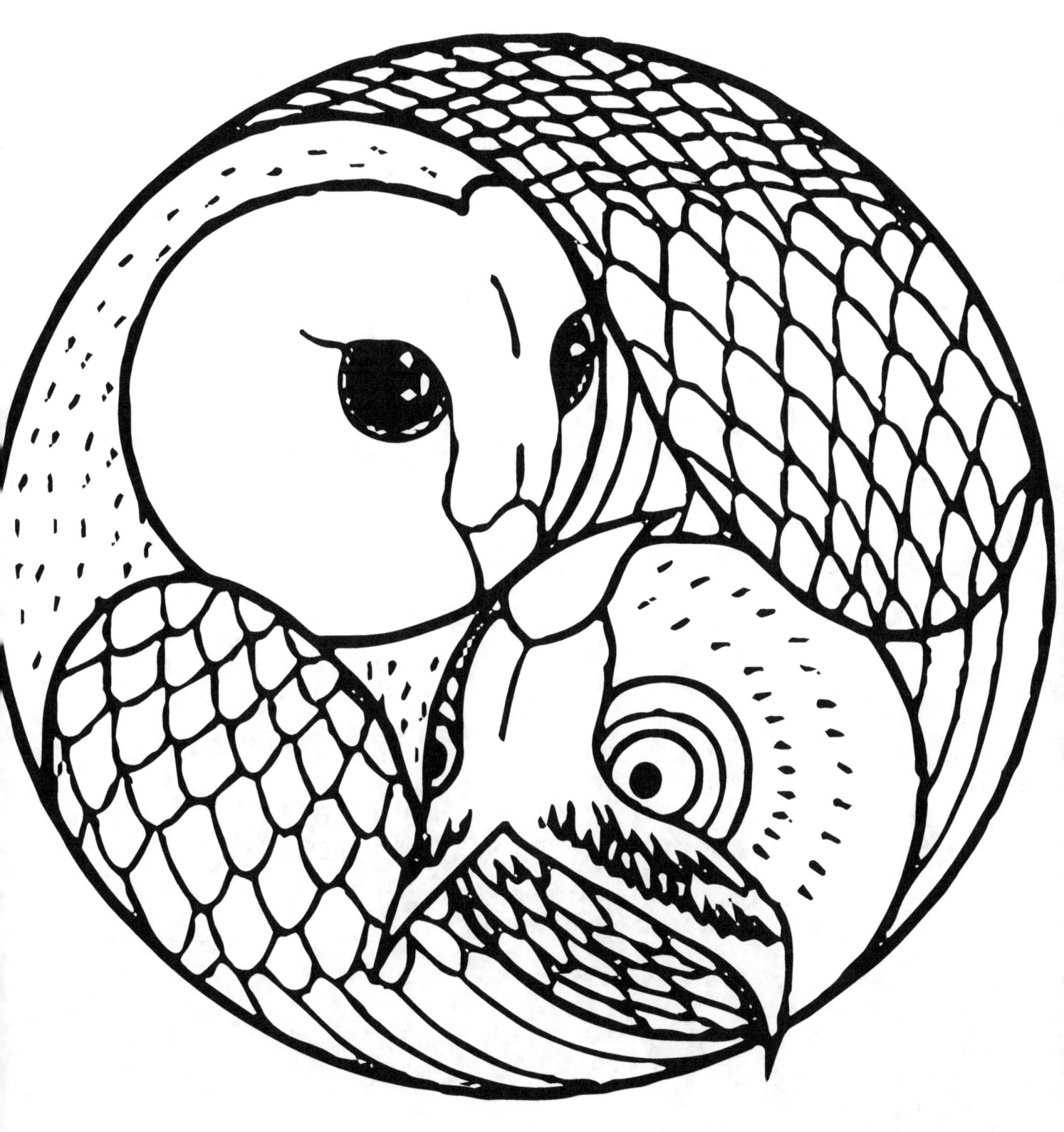

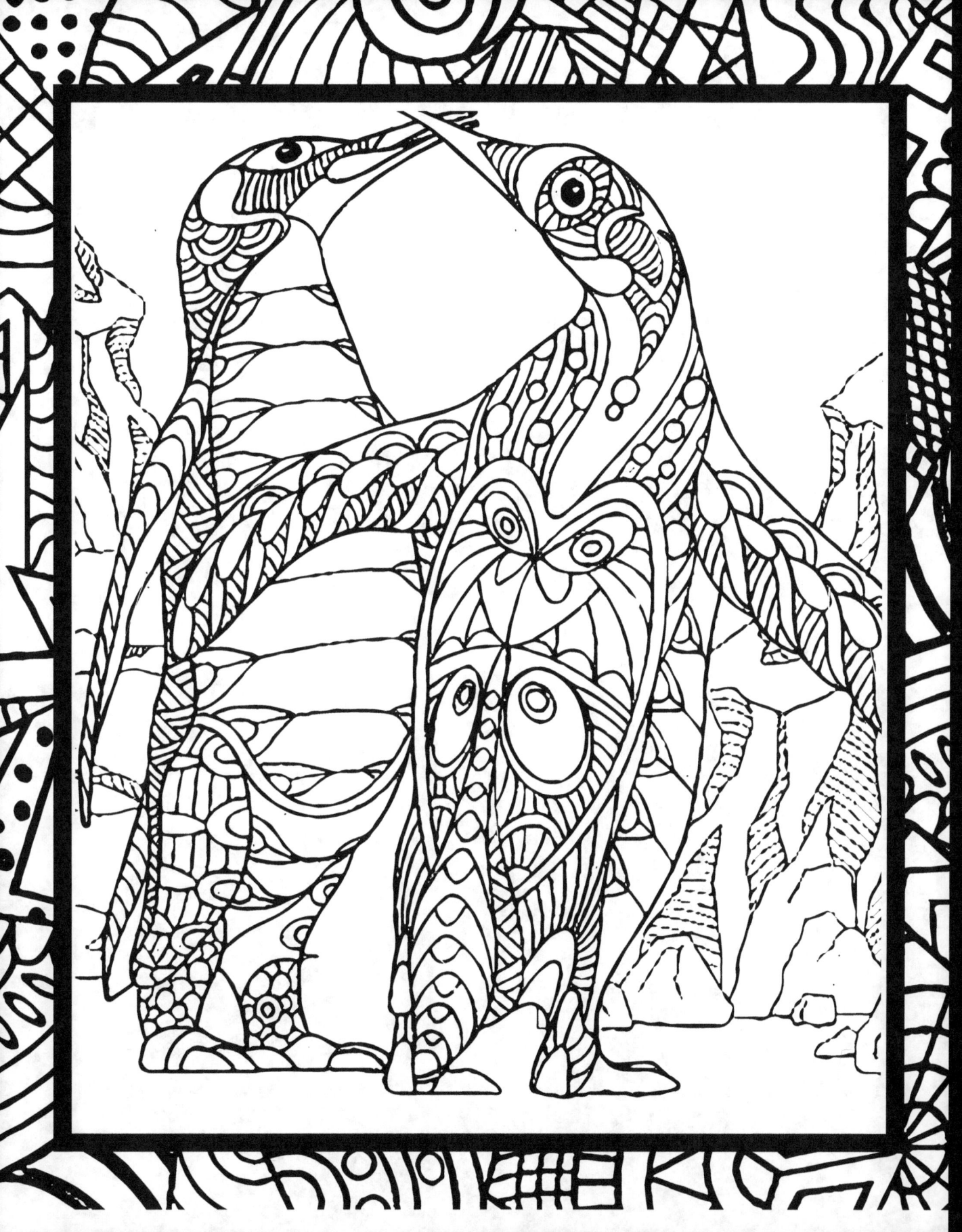

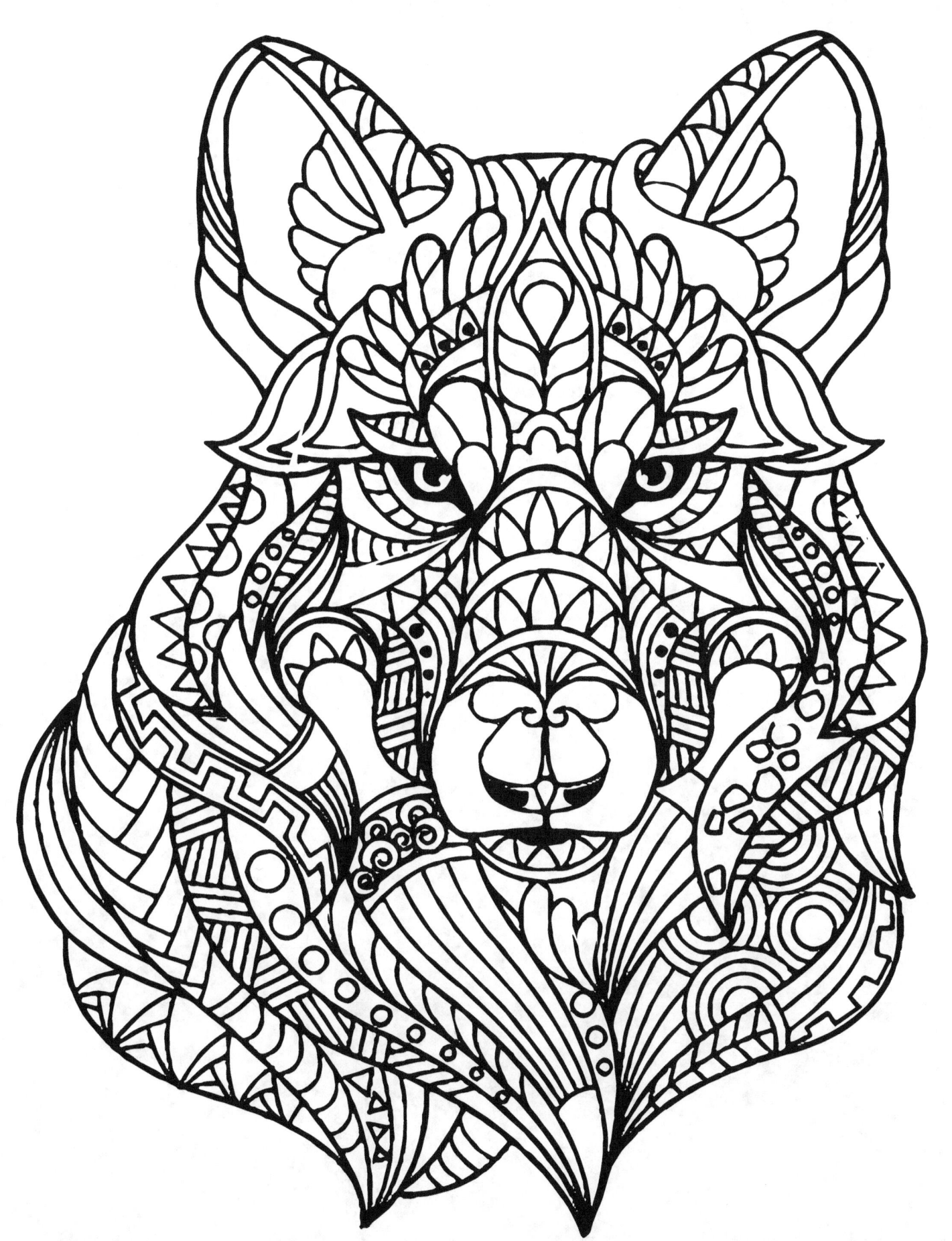

If you liked this book leave us a review

PLEASE

Thank you for buying an authorized edition
of this book. this method is for entertainment use,
so you can have fun, don't take it wrong
.

Invecruz Partner edition supports copyright
protection.Copyright stimulates creativity,
defends diversity in the field
of ideas and knowledge.

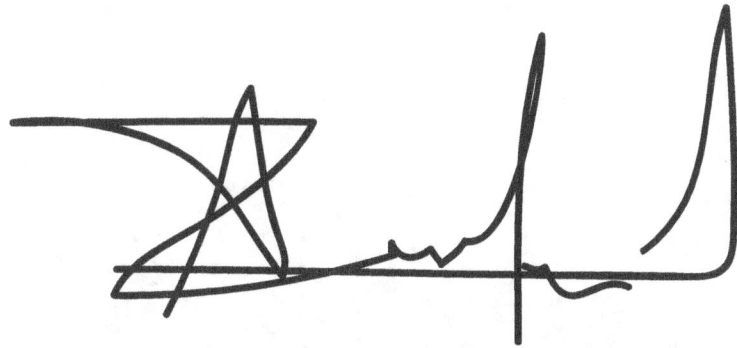

Arthur Little

www.ingramcontent.com/pod-product-compliance
Lightning Source LLC
Chambersburg PA
CBHW060441220526
45465CB00008B/3228